WE NEVER SPEAK OF IT

ALSO BY JANA HARRIS

POETRY

Pin Money
The Clackamas
Manhattan as a Second Language
The Sourlands
Oh How Can I Keep on Singing? Voices of Pioneer Women
The Dust of Everday Life, An Epic Poem of the Pacific Northwest

NOVELS

Alaska
The Pearl of Ruby City

CHAPBOOKS

This House That Rocks with Every Truck on the Road (poetry)
The Book of Common People (poetry)
Who's That Pushy Bitch (poetry)
Family Matters (fiction)

POEMS ADAPTED FOR THE STAGE

Fair Sex (a play by Lynn Middleton based on the poems of
    Jana Harris)
Oh How Can I Keep on Singing? (adapted for the stage by
    Daniel Aubrey from the book by the same title)

POEMS ADAPTED FOR TELEVISION AND VIDEO

How Can I Keep on Singing? (adapted by Moving Images,
    Melissa Young and Mark Dworkin from the book *Oh How
    Can I Keep on Singing?*)

WE NEVER SPEAK OF IT

IDAHO-WYOMING POEMS, 1889-90

Jana Harris

Ontario Review Press ✦ Princeton, NJ

Ontario Review Press
9 Honey Brook Drive
Princeton, NJ 08540

Distributed by W. W. Norton & Co.
500 Fifth Avenue
New York, NY 10110

Library of Congress Cataloging-in-Publication Data

Harris, Jana.
   We never speak of it : Idaho-Wyoming poems, 1889–90 /
   Jana Harris. — 1st ed.
     p. cm.
   ISBN 0-86538-109-7 (alk. paper)
    1. Frontier and pioneer life—Poetry. 2. Women pioneers—
Poetry. 3. Wyoming—Poetry. 4. Idaho—Poetry. I. Title.

   PS3558.A6462W4 2003
   811'.54—dc21

                                              2002193141
First Edition

This is a work of poetry. This is a work of fiction. This is a work of non-fiction. Some of the characters' names have been changed. Some of the characters have been given names when none were supplied. Though there exists a Cottonwood, Idaho, the Cottonwood of this narrative is mythical. All of the events herein are real.

ACKNOWLEDGMENTS: Some of these poems previously appeared in: *The Ontario Review* ("Lemon Pie," "I Drive You from my Heart," "Swans"), *The Clackamas Literary Review* ("Lesson Three: Total Eclipse of the Sun," "The Inclement Weather of the Heart"), *Story Quarterly* ("Monday Afternoon, A Quarter Past Three to a Quarter Past Four"), *Beloit Poetry Journal* ("Broomshop Regulations"), *Prairie Schooner* ("Woman Pausing on the Side of the Road to Tie Her Shoe," "How Sparrows Learn to Spell," "That Springtime of Her Life," "Will They Bar Me at the Gate," "Wrapped in Quilts, Brought Around the Horn, Carried by Wagon to Beyond Boise"), *Hanging Loose* ("Two for a Penny: Counting My Rat Hunting Money," "Nothing but the Blood," "Sixth Grade Composition: Why We Came Here," "Sums and Debits," "What Trees Know"), *The Pushcart Prize Anthology* ("I Drive You From My Heart").

The author wishes to thank the following individuals for their help: K. E. Ellingson, Raymond Smith, Robin Straus, Susan Welch, Suzanne Lebsock, Carol Bower, Trevor Bond, Vicki Lindner, Chris Blomquist, Kristin Kinsey, Mary Brandon, Donald Blanchard M.D., Mark Bothwell, Phil Roberts, Janice Harris.

For the friends of my wild Oregon youth:
Mary Kaczenski Brandon, Kathy Ellingson, Don Blanchard, Denny
Auld; the accident of our paths crossing has been my good fortune—JH

CONTENTS

Crossing Lava Creek *(Annabelle Nelson, 1889)*   13

Lesson Three: Total Eclipse of the Sun *(Mrs. Stanton, 1889)*   16

Sunday Afternoon, A Quarter Past Three to a Quarter Past Four *(Mrs. Stanton, 1889)*   20

Will They Bar Me at the Gate? *(Cassie Hobst, 1889)*   21

Woman Pausing on the Side of the Road to Tie Her Shoe *(Mrs. Stanton, 1889)*   24

Wrapped in Quilts, Brought Around the Horn, Carried by Wagon to Beyond Boise *(Mary Hannah Clark, 1889)*   26

How Sparrows Learn to Spell *(Mrs. Stanton, 1889)*   29

Because Your Backslidings Are Many, Your Transgressions More Than a Few *(Mrs. Stanton, 1889)*   33

Broomshop Regulations *(Duke Deneke, 1889)*   35

Lemon Pie *(Cassie Hobst, 1889)*   38

When Papa Sells the Horses *(Charlie Hobst, 1889)*   43

Every Time Rory Shaughnessy Goes Underground *(Rory Shaughnessy, 1889)*   47

Feeding My New Son with an Eyedropper *(Pauline Krueger, 1889)*   50

What Trees Know *(Cassie Hobst, 1889)*   54

Nothing But the Blood *(Mrs. Stanton, 1889)*   56

Sums and Debits *(Mrs. Stanton, 1889)*   59

How Hard I Try *(Lucy Annie Smith, 1889)*   62

Comes Now Said Defendant *(Mr. Smith, 1889)*   66

Swans *(Mrs. Stanton, 1889)*   69

The Inclement Weather of the Heart *(Mrs. Stanton, 1889)*   72

Borrowed Horses *(Duke Deneke, 1889)*   74

That Springtime of Her Life *(Mrs. Stanton, 1890)*   82

Two for a Penny: Counting My Rat-Hunting Money
   (Mary Hannah Clark, 1890)   84

I Have Always Believed It Is Entirely Possible to Pray While
   Chopping Wood *(Martha James, 1890)*   87

I Drive You from My Heart *(Mrs. Stanton, 1890)*   90

Sixth Grade Composition: Why We Came Here *(Jarvis Fisher,
   1890)*   94

Ante-Over the Outside Bissy *(Annabelle Nelson, 1890)*   97

We Never Speak of It   *(Mrs. Stanton, 1890)*   99

Afterword   103

Credits: Map, Photographs   111

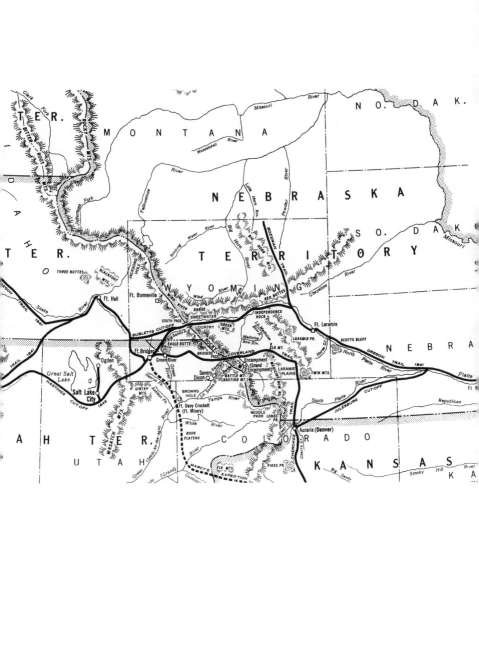

CROSSING LAVA CREEK
Annabelle Nelson, Age 11
Cottonwood School House, 1889

April,
a freakish storm came up.

At breakfast, father said:
wolves seen in Lava Creek.
On my way to school I tiptoed
down, across, up the other side
so no wolf would hear me.
My feet never froze
—mother knitted woolen stockings,
father tanned hides, a lot of work,
making moose skin moccasins.

After lunch, thin clouds
dark as creosote
blackened the air.
We'd no lanterns, only
one candle. Teacher sent two
older boys to fetch kindling,
corn cobs, anything.
The boys stampeded for home.
Light dimmed. I wanted to leave, but
those wolves. A boat
—the upside-down woodshed roof—
pitched across the sky.
Teacher called for recess in the cellar
playing singing games.
I sang loud, sucking in
mouthfuls of mousy air, thinking
of the boys who'd bolted.
(Was I the only one to notice
teacher praying?)
I sat on the ladder—stand up
and I had to stoop—stomped
to music, *Oh happy day*

that fixed my course brought
to mind the boat roof flying by.
Mice ran across my feet—
in tallowy light,
younger children's faces
white as candle wax. Some held their ears.
Shutterbang, ventwhistle, shingles clat-
tered off the roof. A hail
of corn snow. *Oh happy bond*
that sealed my vows.

The white robe of Jesus
covered rows of desks upstairs,
the stove a ghostly mound of snow.
Outside: trees uprooted, cordwood
scattered everywhere. *Let only happy*
anthems fill this house, we sang, carried
forty buckets of snow outside.
Teacher said, Jesus filled the shed roof boat
with a cargo of angels' wings. Before dark,
fathers finally came, some cried
to see their children still alive.

Crossing Lava Creek,
fresh wolf tracks in the snow.

LESSON THREE:
TOTAL ECLIPSE OF THE SUN
Frances Stanton, Cottonwood, Idaho, 1889

Lesson one: How to do Pineapple—
Showed the wild looking,
never-seen-before thing.
Asked, what is it?
Thorns, leafy spikes,
perfume of peach pie.
Asked, what to do?
Cut deep under peeling and
pare away, dethorn,
halve, core by triangle
incision, slice.

Cottonwood, capital
of Idaho's wide empty scablands.
Most older boys
never had schooling and
lived in tents. To them
I was a women with an oven and
the only home with a clock.
Many had homemade sundials, few
children taught how to read them.
No log house, my new address;
bedrooms, papered parlor,
plenty of windows. Running water
in the spring fifteen feet
from my door. My stove,
fueled by sage, scorched everything.
Like everyone else,
our Christmas tree
was a five-foot tall
tumbleweed.

Next to the Stage Stop,
one general store without milk, eggs
or greens, not even
potatoes among the hanging
carcasses of sheep, bins
of hardware, horse shoes,
hammer heads.
Dry Creek prowled
by diamondbacks and
bobcats while mud wallows
harbored yellow jackets.

Arithmetic Lesson with Orange:
gently peeled, set aside rind
for kitchen use. Exhibited:
The Whole with its many equal parts,
the smallest natural portion,
one-twelfth the sphere.
On flat of my hand, held out sections for
call and response—number,
name of fraction. Next question:
what part half a section?
Awarded one twenty-fourth to each scholar.
Extra pieces to the child
who stoked the fire,
filled the water pail, cleaned
my fleece erasers.

Science Lesson:
placed tin washtub
on plank desk, poured enough
water in to capture sun's reflection,
explained why it was eaten
by moonshadow, causing
hens to roost, milkers to wander
in from the canyon as

17

darkness crossed
the juniper dotted lava fields and
sow belly plains, rolling up
dry grass benchlands
ribboned by willows lining creeks.
Eerie silence followed, broken
by mourning doves, a calf
crying for its cow, coyote
wail, fire crackle.
For comfort,
rubbed sage, pealed away bark.

Here ends the lesson.

SUNDAY AFTERNOON, A QUARTER PAST
THREE TO A QUARTER PAST FOUR
Frances Stanton, Cottonwood, Idaho, 1889

It was after I poked up the fire, sat down, began to pare
and core apples that you—gone, unheard of, not thought
about in years—appeared at the door. You spoke your
name. I thought, a stage stop somewhere? Just a word at
first that, like yourself, carried no baggage. And now you
sit at my table, a man who might have been my husband—
you even look like the one I married, though your face has
silvered, your head tousled with salt. You spread out three
decades as dispassionately as you spread a napkin across
your lap, reciting dates, numbers of cattle, market value,
year by year. In 1868 a marriage, later a woman's name
falls, like my paring knife, into our conversation. Your
wife? Her people's ranch? My questions are lost in your
litany of railroads, miles covered, horseshoes lost, the price
of flathead nails, hinges. When you ask about my life, you
don't mean each heartbreak, each baby never born. Your
children? No names given, all girls, married, gone;
somewhere a new grandchild: weight, length, name not
supplied. Suddenly hot tears brand my cheeks. You ask,
can you lend sympathy? Sympathy? For thirty wordless
years? How is it I care more about you now than as a maid
of fifteen? I reply, No, witless of me, thank you: I've
peeled, pared, peeled again an onion instead of a Winesap.
In my dishpan float a dozen cored apples, wheels without
hubs, circles without centers. The sweet tarts I promise will
never satisfy what is empty within me.
　　I watch you eat your fill, ride on.

WILL THEY BAR ME AT THE GATE?
Cassie Hobst, age 6, Cottonwood, Idaho, 1889

Last Sunday, Reverend said, Husband
be not afraid to wade into the water
to save your wife. Woman,
be not afraid to wade after your spouse.
Later Mumma asked,
did I know how many times
she had to walk into deep water
to save me in just one day? *Did I?*
Will they bar me at The Gate,
Mumma says, should be
my every waking moment's worry.
Just look at Dolly, what a neglectful
little mother I am, my only begotten
hasn't a foot and her face is filthy.
Innocence always suffers,
Mumma says. Sit still, Cassie.
And I do, my fleshy ways halted
on the veranda's apple crate stairstep. How
can I trust your heart? Mumma asks.
My many transgressions, my knack
for doing evil. Who's she talking to?
I question Dolly, swinging her
by raggedy legs, smashing
her corn husk hair
against the porch rail so that
one of her eyes pops off.
If Mumma did not have her hands
and arms and elbows in snow
drifts of raw misery lye soap,
she would crown me with her Bible
opened to Romans.

"Armored by Light," Cassie,
"Go into the house and come back out
Armored by Light." So
I retrieve Dolly's red button eye
faded to pink from dust,
grab the Siwash-made spruceroot
sewing basket, hold
my thimbled thumb to the sun.
Harm-ed by Light, Mumma, here I come,
Harmed by Light.

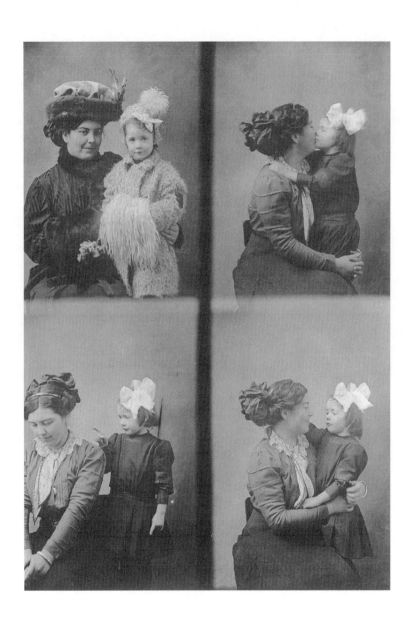

WOMAN PAUSING ON THE SIDE OF
THE ROAD TO TIE HER SHOE
Frances Stanton, Cottonwood, Idaho, 1889

It is written: where your treasure is,
your heart be also, but
a broken shoelace shouldn't make me weep.
Easier to gather grapes from buckthorn
figs from purple thistle flower than
dispel this inner darkness.
What is it they tell children
while thrashing hazelnut switches
in front of cracked faces: *stop blubbering*
before I give you something to cry about?
Where's the treasure amid a landscape
as featureless as oatmeal,
endless oven-hot winds and ice pick rocks?
Dust in my shoes, behind my collar. And beneath me,
razoring through a dry river of brown
bent grass like the hair of the dead, a snake.
What was it mother used to say...*cried because*
I had no shoes until I met a man who had no feet.
And when you lose the secret shelf your soul sits on,
where's the silver lining then? What's worse than this
drum rolling electrical storm of the self?
The sting of November's never-ceasing rain,
a phlegm-gray sky for months on end?
When did I first look up into the firmament,
seeing holes where stars had been?
How desperate I've become:
My shoestring has broken, the frayed end
undone again and I've no other laces.
My boot flops like a palsied head—
a lolling tongue letting grit steal in, my heel a bed
of pearl blisters. What cleanses the spirit
when Jordan turns brackish?
My neck too weak to hold up my chin.
Bonnet so heavy, I remove

the brim slats, let the bill droop
across my face, a veil shielding my eyes:
I imagine that small snake's
dark serpentine the shade-cooled
milk and honeyed Hallelujah shore of my youth.

Stand up, Mrs. Stanton. Stand and tie your shoe.
You ask for bread, here is a stone;
you ask for fish, here is a serpent. But
many rocks piled will build you a house;
even ravenous wolves fear the tiniest snake.
Where your treasure is, your heart be also.

WRAPPED IN QUILTS, BROUGHT AROUND THE HORN, CARRIED BY WAGON TO BEYOND BOISE
Mary Hannah Clark, age 14

I turn you upright, place you sideways
over the fireplace mantel, above
a west-facing sun-in-the-afternoon window,
on top of the drygoods box used as a dresser.
Baby wants to see you, but mama says,
bad luck for infants
to be caught in a looking glass.
Father combs his hair.
Mama won't pause in front of you
for fear of losing the courage
to go on. A boy turns his cheek to see
if it needs a good scrubbing.
All the time I secretly scream:
my turn, my turn to place you
above the wash bucket, then
by the back door. Carried outside, where
in the clear light of day you may bespeak
promises unutterable in firelight. I count
the spots on you, *he loves me*
he loves me not. I dress for him.
My heart chokes if a day goes by
without sight of him.
When morning marches in,
in front of you, I pull on a lace scrim
for him, for him. Today
my gray stockings; I point my toe at you,
show them off. Always, I walk to school
so as to cross his path coming home,
overalls mud-caked, from the mine.
All I want is his good opinion.
What he gives me is a small sharp
stone with flecks of mirrory glitter,
the only treasure in my jewelry box.

When he comes to dinner,
mama kills a precious hen,
makes ice cream trying not to think
of the butter she could have sold.
To please *him* I try not to say "darn."
While our mothers visit,
he helps with dishes, snatching
the towel, teaching me to clean
fry pans by putting them in the fire.
His breath smells of cloves;
a bad sign, mama tells me later and
it is you I run to.
You say *pretty*, he does not.
I am overcome with a new kind
of homesickness. Does such trouble
come to any other girl? When I stare at you
in starlight, one thought softens the brittle dark:
the same moon shines on us both, him and me.

I tell mama: I cannot sleep due to headaches.
You know better.

HOW SPARROWS LEARN TO SPELL
A-R-I-T-H-M-E-T-I-C
Frances Stanton, Cottonwood School House, Idaho, 1889

Nameless, they appeared without warning,
a family of four children, the older
having waited until the youngest
legal school age to attend.
Living miles from town, they'd never
heard English. Their tongue,
was it Czech? The town Blacksmith, a Slav,
said it sounded Norwegian.
The mother lived out, doing miners' mending,
no one ever heard tell of their father.
If called upon, I'd swear
they'd brought up themselves. Their language
the chirping of birds. Thus, for their sparrow-
like trills I named them.

The other scholars jeered at their chatter:
Chee-chee: please, please,
a dipper of water;
cheep-cheep: may I sit
a hare's breath closer to the fire.
Having fashioned their own lexicon,
they understood one another. Eventually
I could school them, but only after learning
some of their jargon: *book, book,*
slate, slate. Their classmates helped:
miming letters, concocting word games.

At noon, the sparrows ate—
dinner pails filled with the bread
of worry and water of affliction.
One by one, other scholars shared—
a pat of lard, a heel of rye, a turkey quill pen.

Nights, I kept all four after class.
One thought "Punishment"
both his given and surname.
The youngest so bashful,
when forbidden to peep,
uttered not a whisper.
Worse, another stuttered.
Greasing her speech
tried my soul and my patience.

It is said: when a lamp shines in darkness,
darkness does not understand. But
as if making a trap with a loop of cord
to entangle their feet,
I managed to ensnare them and slowly
my sparrows learned to spell and to sing:

A Rat In The House Might Eat The Ice Cream

BECAUSE YOUR BACKSLIDINGS ARE MANY, YOUR TRANSGRESSIONS MORE THAN A FEW

Frances Stanton intones "The Parable of the Two Sheep & the Wise Shepherd," Cottonwood Schoolhouse, Idaho, 1889

Once a wise shepherd called his charges in order to count them and after all came running discovered two extra sheep standing at the head of his flock. Any ordinary shepherd would have rejoiced at such a blessing, thinking himself suddenly wealthier. But our wise shepherd knew that the first sheep was really a wolf hungry for sheep. Anyone but a sheep could see this. The second sheep was a goat hungry for the fodder of sheep. The second sheep's true identity was not so easy to detect. It had dung-colored eyes with irises shaped like tabletops. The first sheep had a long snout and canine teeth and dung-colored eyes with irises shaped like tabletops.

When the creator put the cunning wolf upon the earth on the sixth day, he commanded this prowler of the evening to gnaw the bones of meeker creatures to the marrow. When the creator put the clever goat upon the earth on the sixth day, he sentenced this daytime chewer of the cud to gnaw rough herbage. These two counterfeit sheep were not destined to meet, should they not have coveted the tender taste of fleece or the soft pasture that produced it.

Class, if I were to ask you to recite the Lesson of the Wise Shepherd, you might respond: a wise shepherd remembers that when counting his blessings, the wolves of judgment and the goats of treachery run before sheep. And what more could we say if this tale were put under the lens of further scrutiny? That before passing judgment, the cunning wolf waits until the treacherous goat has eaten the very grass beneath his shepherd's feet? Possibly, possibly; but the moral is: envy not the blessing of sudden riches to others, as it may be no blessing at all.

BROOMSHOP REGULATIONS
Duke Deneke, Rawlins, Wyoming, 1889

Dear Ma'am,
Just to inform you
I have four more months
to accomplish my end.
Here I tie brooms, not the best job—
which would be working
the tailor shop or kitchen.
Today: we had plenty of drinking water.
Back when the first tints of green
began to show despite cold nights, I cursed
all sheep and anything to do with their evil
smelling wooly puff faces, then eloped
with a saddle, coming back
for a different man's horse;
a long heavy Colt contraption
essential to my future.
You often basted me about whiskey, but
one drink turns me top heavy for hours,
though a square pink bottle of hatchwood rye
—rat poison really—good health
insurance against snakebite.
And if that don't work, mix it with coal oil
kept for building fires in wet sage during
lambing time. Always open season
on horse thieves and herders—a hot metal
slug passed so close to my face it rendered me
deaf, dizzy, and common as these
rust-coated eating utensils here

where even the broomshop is dusty
enough to bring on quick consumption.
Tying, not such hard work, but
tiresome standing all day.
So hungry by ten sometimes I eat
broom corn. Others eat soap to get

out of knotting their quota which
never works and I've never known anyone
to return from the veterinary's infirmary.
Bet the skeleton that decorates the corner
of your schoolroom came from here. I've started
to chew tobacco with the good effect
of it making me so sick
my stomach forgets to gnaw. At night
if unshackled, we're permitted
to make horsehair hackamores by lamplight.
We're permitted paper and ink once a week.
We're permitted to talk at meals
three times a year:
Thanksgiving, Christmas, Fourth of July.
Ma'am, if I am overly weary of anything
it is of hard crusts and ends of loaves,
stew one morning, hash the next,
thin soup at three. Every Monday
I carve my brand into an old bread heel,
on Friday it's still in the bread pan.
I heard a guard tell a visitor we'd be
uncontrollable if ever
we got enough to eat.

You often said I'd be hanged
before I turned twenty-one.
I'm writing to say
I've four more months
to prove you wrong.

Souvenir

Greetings and
Best Wishes
from Your Teacher

LEMON PIE
Cassie Hobst, age 6, Cottonwood, Idaho, 1889

Something about the smell of heat,
something about the tepid
sun-gone light of mosquito hour
and nettly insect stings
burning my arms as I ran in
from the orchard carrying
a lard bucket of cherries,
made me ask Mumma,
Why'd Lazarus wanna rise up
from the dead?
The Bible teaches
what the Bible teaches, Mumma said,
wiping sweat pearls off her brow.
Waiting for temperatures to break,
Mumma promised lemon pie, but
we hadn't citrus and now only dead hens, so
pie cherry vinegar pie would have to do.

Mumma thought I could go to school
a year early. People today, she said,
never learn their nursery rhymes.
Disruptive, a new word to everyone.
Sent home for a spell, I pick cherries,
three varieties. Piebald calves and a pig
grazing beneath the orchard ladder. That boar's
blunt snorts like filthy words:
knock you off, knock you off...
Hurling nut-shaped stones,
I tweaked his ear.
Now I'd get it. Never before hit
anything I'd aimed at, this time
Oinker fell over dead.
A dunce hat girl and
a pig killer all in one week.

Meals on time, meals on time
makes a nursery rhyme.
Always water aboil.
I wasn't awfully good with livestock
—a dead boar in the orchard,
living proof—so I never got to rodeo
cattle. Mumma said,
holding potato peelers, good practice
for my pencil grip. Save all
feathers when you butcher hens.
Five birds to a pillow; a ten-pullet stew pot,
how many pillows, Cassie?
But Mumma, Piggy's sleeping too close
to the orchard ladder's hooves.
Cherry fed bacon's the best, Mumma said.

Never knew where I'd sleep till night.
And if I should wake before I die...
Uncles had their own beds,
children didn't, buckaroos dozed
on hardwood by the fire,
children on splintery kitchen planks
near the stove. First light, through
dawn's no-see-em flies and the smell
of willow pollen, I carried
a washboard behind
Mumma and the aunts down creek
where iron tubs boiled and boiled
the rodeo men's breeches. Uncles' meals
came first, even on laundry day,
a ten pullet soup stovetop.
Mumma said, Cassie, go ladle up.

And I said, Piggy's still asleep
—didn't move even when a devil's funnel
struck the branding pen, black
corral dust stealing the house,
chinking slack enough so sand shot through
like sewing pins stabbing
the soup, the melty butter,
peppering clabbered milk hung up
to drain in little sugar sacks—
now only fit for pig slop.
Someone's sure to notice. No soup,
no butter biscuits, no lemon pie
—which mother had promised—
but heat snakes had turned
the cherry-pit vinegar almost ripe.

It took two shifts to feed;
not enough dishes, beans, beef; but
the uncles' mouths turned up
in happy fish hooks at the hope
of Lemon Pie.

When one curd-faced buckaroo fell,
broke his leg, Father took the door off
the house to carrying him to wagon.
Our town? Hardware, coal yard,
the undertaker our furniture maker, coffins
came from there. If a stage stop
had a mortician then
there had to be a doctor—
though no nursery rhyme assures this.

No time to confess. Auntie sews
faster than her voice scratches
the dove-colored air. When she sent
me back to the orchard—
more cherries for relish, anything
to cover the briny taste of dust soup—
flies like raisins on the boar's china-pink ears,
I ran backwards, scream-singing
Piggy's dead, piggy's dead...
Mince venison, not words, Mumma said.
Just then, Oinker rose on wobbly pegs,
staggered away. That night, no forgiveness
for lemon pie lies in the Book of Luke.
The Bible teaches what the Bible teaches.
When she made up my bed
on the pine plank floor, I whispered,

Mumma, I know what Lazarus died of.

WHEN PAPA SELLS THE HORSES
Charlie Hobst Lectures His Younger Brothers and Sisters
Open Range Country, Idaho/Wyoming, 1889

When Papa sells the horses,
he'll bring me red copper-toed boots,
no matter how much I shuffle,
I cannot wear them out.
He'll bring you a porcelain doll with real hair
to braid, he'll bring you licorice,
a ball that bounces high as the barn.
When Papa sells the mares and foals,
he'll buy machinery to clear more land,
he'll buy cattle, a gun; we won't be a place
that raises some chickens, mainly coyotes—
we won't be people who have only rocks
and calluses to show for all our work.

When Papa sells the saddle horses
we'll have paper tablets to practice
our script and sums instead
of the frosted window for a slate.
We'll not eat bull elk
until our insides stiffen with grease,
we'll not have to eat
dropped food from the floor.

When Papa sells the broncs and yearlings
we'll ride in a buggy, not
a heavy jolting wagon—little brother
clinging to mama's hem
wailing to drown out the baby.
Papa'll buy a buggy, take us to Oregon's
sea of wheat fields and plum
orchards white blossoming in butterflies;
Oregon, where there's so much antelope meat
waste is a sin will be hard to remember,
where Papa will have time of an evening

to whittle me a ship in a bottle.
When Papa sells the fillies and colts,
we'll not be left here without him,
at night in our bedrolls
all children covered in sage ticks
that look like moles and so tattooed
in mosquito bites mama has to
bandage us in baking soda.

When Papa sells his horses broke to harness,
he'll come home, fix the catch on the door
so it'll close without being slammed.
He'll solder a new handle for the kettle,
solder every bucket and pot
that's got tiny holes plugged shut with cloth.

When Papa sells the horses broke to ride
We'll not have to worry about diphtheria,
scarlet fever, typhoid: the three plagues.
When Papa sells the horses broke to plow
we'll have money for the doctor and mama
won't fret about burying her children
amid rock and sage like animals where
even God himself could not find us
on Resurrection Day.

When Papa sells the blue ribbon mare,
he'll not send us letters with promises
of a present at Christmas, lots of x's
and o's and news that though
no one is buying horses, still
they must be fed.
When Papa sells the stallion,
mama will not have to keep
her forceps handy for pulling
people's teeth at fifty cents apiece,
or trade away our butter and eggs
for livestock salt.

No one's forgetting,
when Papa sells the herd:
our cup of happiness full for days,
all our hard times behind us.
When papa sells the horses,
he'll have time to whittle me
a creek-willow whistle,
whittle himself a pipe.
When Papa sells the horses,
he'll whittle tiny parts of a tiny ship in a bottle,
which, he says, is just like life:
all the bitty pieces done right or you'll ruin it.

EVERY TIME RORY SHAUGHNESSY
GOES UNDERGROUND
**Empress Sylvia Mine
near Cottonwood, 1889**

The feeling of being buried,
the feeling of dampness, the drone
of dripping water, the smell of burned powder,
bad air, a stomach that feels as if
it's swallowed a flat iron.
The special feel of darkness, dirt
shifting under rotting timbers, rats
shifting under rotting timbers. Fear
of carelessness, of a co-worker
with more bear grease than brains,
of a drunken engineer new to graveyard shifts
—the different hours of eating and sleeping—
stepping out of a drift, missed footing,
falling into the shaft across the bucket.

Imagining the world above: the safety of home.
On every kitchen stove pieces of ore roasting.
Water poured over hot rocks forcing out
blisters the shape of yellow coins.
Every step mud and sludge, water and ice.
Every man with a piece of quartz he tongues
to show specks of heaven.
Samples from the latest blast hauled up.
A strike? The mining bug. Better than
wearing out heart and shoe leather
searching for work. Wondering why
some prosper and get along while others
do not—some so lucky even their horses kick up
ore-bearing quartz on the trail.

Sweat pours. A full day's work done
on a half-cooked breakfast, then
a long run from mine to stream
and stamp mill—like a giant
iron potato masher—the crush running
over plates coated with quicksilver,
noise deafening as cardrooms full of men
crying and singing drunk.

Walking home, someone plays
the mouth harp. Summer comes late.

FEEDING MY NEW SON WITH AN EYEDROPPER, I REMEMBER COMING TO THIS COUNTRY WITH MY PARENTS, ONE TRUNK, AND SEVEN WORDS OF ENGLISH

Pauline Krueger, Open Range Country,
Idaho/Wyoming, 1889

Until he moved, I knew nothing
about him and almost the next week
it seemed he wanted to be born.
Alone, too soon, what could I do
but wrap him in cotton batting—
even in America, one does not name
a child marked for death.
Bottle and nipple clumsy contraptions,
too big for his mouth, I had to
draw back his lip, spoon in
nature's nourishment. His shoulders
nonexistent, legs shriveled—how did I manage
to mark him so?

Still all newborns bring
their own welcome—he looks
as alien as I did when first
I came to this county:
my funny name (papa immediately
dropped its harsher vowels),
my funny dress, shoes
clumsy as cod boxes.
My hair braided wet, brushed
until it stood out like a broom.
New York City.
The first American word I learned
was *hurry*, the second, *fifth floor walkup*.
That troublesome *th*, putting tongue
against teeth made a sound
of geese hissing, recalled
the Von's white flock.

In the old country we owned only
the goose's feathers and eggs, never
its liver. My brothers never dreamed
of owning the horses they curried.
We carried our clod hopper shoes to church,
so that our heels wouldn't wear.
When the boys went to school, receiving primers,
I read the Von's old newspapers.

Every store in Manhattan
owned by royalty—*greenhorn,*
what did it mean? Mama—wanting me
to fit in—bought me (I'd never before
seen coin money) a green silk blouse.
Trading my fishbox shoes for narrow
pointy-toed boots, piling my hair
on my head modishly, I went to market
with my coins, my new name, new blouse,
and my seven words of English
which no one could understand; so pointed
at one of a bewildering array of vegetables.
I had no word for *yellow cucumber*
and until that day had never known
the word or fruit I bought—*banana.*

Sweetened potato water, bread
soaked in milk, nothing agrees with baby.
Not that we had food to spare, but
always room for one more and soon wonder
how I managed to get along without him.
Husband still away, it grieves me to pray
alone, but God never blows the wind
harder than you can stand. Busy hands make
a busy mind, I whittle a thread spool
into a top, three spools make a teething ring,
a cigar box and four spools, a wagon,
baking powder tin half full of buttons, baby's rattle;
but he shows no interest in toys
and looks a thousand years old.

Squirming out of his clothes,
too tiny to be dressed, he sleeps
hours on end, never cries, will not nurse.
When the clock tells me
uncover and feed,
I expect to find him dead.
Sleep with him, keep him
in the bread warmer, finally
tiny limbs begin to fill in.
When at last I let myself
think he'll live, I worry:
Dear Lord, if there is any fault
let it be in body, not in brain.
So much hoped for and all we have
this year is a crippled baby

But with a sunny disposition,
and even before he tries to walk
can mimic on the mouth harp
what he hears a fiddler play.
Now his rattle makes a soul-satisfying sound
and he chews anything he can get a hold of,
sprouting teeth at an alarming rate.
At noon, at midnight, together
with the clock's hands pointed
upward in a prayerful position,
I entreat in German so as not to tax God
with my terrible English: *Bitte,*
give me strength to be the one
tenderness between baby and this wilderness.

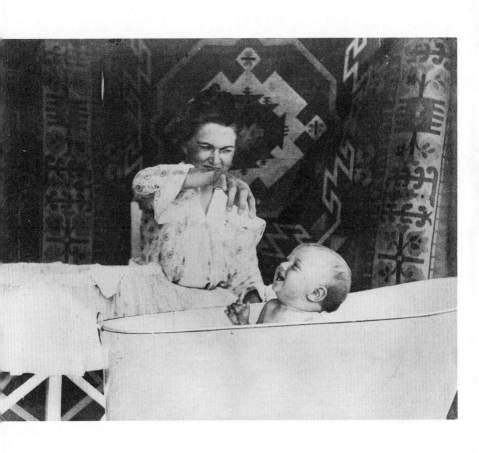

WHAT TREES KNOW
When Tilden and Cassie are Sent Home From School Early
Cassie Hobst, age almost seven
Cottonwood, Idaho, 1889

I tell the calf and new litter
of pigs, mostly spotted
four more white than black:
Tis a simple rule to remember:
Two to a desk, girls on this side
boys on that.

Thrashing a handbell,
I bang my new ruler three times against
the barn fence, calling
my charges to class:
If you cannot read,
if you speak in lisping voices,
if you do not learn your numbers,
you will quietly crochet.
No wiggling. Or whispering.
Raise a hand to speak.
Show respect: stand,
arms behind you. Answer:
yes ma'am and no ma'am. Now

who will lead the flag pledge,
recite a verse of scripture?
I whack my ruler against the fence post,
against a piggy's pearly butt.
Miss Teacher's measuring stick,
foot long, yea wide, real thin.
Today at school, Tilden wore
her ruler's print across his ear
red as rhubarb, a white welt rising.
With a nail I scratch spelling words
into the cow manger. The north

side of the granary my blackboard,
number problems already etched there:
one plus one equals what?
The answer much excites the chickens
who like my teaching.

Father does not.
Cassie, he says, under no uncertain terms
is a barn a blackboard. Do you understand
the word *for-bidden*?

I move my classroom
to the orchard. There are things
you cannot teach a pig.
Apple trees are better learners
they nod, they let me dance with them,
they do not spank as I will not
if I am teacher. Unlike father,
I will tell everything you can't
and should not do.
Trees, I say, whacking
my new ruler against a trunk:
If you butcher a pig when he is angry,
it's a bloody mess,
the meat, never good, and the fat
foams in the pan.

No one raises a branch.
No one has to tell trees the rules, because
trees are not troublemakers.
Trees are always, always, *always*
mute and docile and good.

"NOTHING BUT THE BLOOD," SINGING LESSON
Frances Stanton, Cottonwood Schoolhouse, 1889

Every time the Snake leaps
its banks, even well water physics me.
Sugar of lead and blue moss
bring no effect.
My young scholars complain,
cannot sit upright or sing
at their desks. I keep laudanum
in the grub box, dab water of bluestone
on thrushy mouths while
Nothing but the blood... Cassie
stares relentlessly out the door
at potato-colored rocks and prairie dog holes.
Tilden has tied ornaments
in his hair mimicking a Blackfoot, and I
can think of nothing but
What can wash away my sin?
my exhaustion and the fact
that tonight I must bake yeast bread then...
What can make me whole again?
Mosquitoes so terrible,
even inside the schoolhouse
we hear cattlestomp. Took
a single dose of quinine this a.m.,
feel some better. When
I asked the time of day, Cassie said,
"from the shadows, I'd judge..."
From the clock, I corrected, but
still she cannot read its face.
For my cleansing, this my plea...
Annabelle frets from earaches.
Claire's actions have her running
for the necessary house. Passed
a tapeworm, thought her intestines
had come inside out.

Tilden complains of a sore face
due to decayed teeth, an excuse
for authoring mischief?
For my pardon, this I seek...
But ten lashes changes nothing,
and once when I gave him twenty, he cried
so bitterly: ten his age, oughtn't I to stop
at ten? *Nothing but the blood of Jesus...*
My only joy in that he could count.
By noon, heat and dust—
dust worse than wind
or wood ticks, like wearing *Nothing*
can for sin atone... a second skin.
Will I ever be clear of the misery of it?
Not even nightfall before I need a bath.
Outside, men at the crossing
urge cattle onto the ferry
which sometimes sinks, sometimes
they are there till dark
driving a single herd across.
Sometimes my scholars seem cattle-brained,
my hands overflowing
Naught of good that I have done... but
with so much sickness and stubbornness that
—*nothing but the blood of Jesus*—
I'm at a loss as to what will make me
white as snow *whole again.*
Blood resolved, I re-set the pitch,
pledge to do right, my pure white duty,
my bright as snow best, and
command the children: *Sing.*

SUMS AND DEBITS
Frances Stanton, Cottonwood, 1889

On top of all my sins
—haste, sloth, gluttony,
taking the Lord's name in vain—this
morning, snow sitting belligerently
on window sills,
the water pitcher frozen.
Walking to the schoolhouse,
my feet shot out from under me,
head striking the hitching post.
Dizzily, I picked up scattered dinner pail
and booksack. A morning when
I wished I didn't have to start the fire
—feeling as if my head had been chopped
by an axe. Carrying ashes from the stove,
spread them across the walk
to prevent further ice-ups—sometimes
getting to class a greater challenge
than teaching. Claire wears no mittens
freezing her fingers so often
the nails have fallen off and she has to
be excused from penmanship. Some,
like Tilden—who today
claims to have magic vision—
put feed sacks over faces,
holes cut for eyes, keeping
the bee stings of cold from cheeks.
After dumping ash, I pile stones
and bricks beneath the stove
to warm the children's feet.
Nausea. The pain almost blinding.
I put my head on my desk.

Sums on the blackboard,
words to spell. Their last teacher
a sawmill owner, the only arithmetic
they know is board feet. Outside,
a constant wind blisters every wall chink.
Little Cassie Hobst says, if you can hear
the American flag flutter,
you knew it's not frozen.
Tilden claims to have
an Indian potion enabling him
to see girl's underthings. I would
give him sore spots to sit on,
if it weren't for this throbbing.
When I lay my head down again,
he follows Cassie to the outhouse,
locking her in. Rising from my desk,
I cannot straighten my back, my neck
a wilted stem. Claire spies
Cassie's red knit scarf dangling from
the bissy's crescent moon and I know
I must right myself, my head swelling up
in a knob. Cassie's feet so numb
she cannot walk. Head pounding.
I drag her like a fawn carcass
across the schoolyard.
Tilden's punishment:
to carry in a day's wood.
I would like to take my ruler,
bang his hands until they color blue as Cassie's
whose mother is called to fetch her.
When Mrs. Hobst exclaims,
"She'll marry that Tilden someday,"
Cassie dares not back-sass.
Malt liquor? Blue ruin?

Attempting to name my illness,
Mrs. Hobst bends toward me.
Temples pulsing and not
up to an arguing match,
I turn to sums and debits,
the reassuring call and response
of: "Class, unlike our sinful selves,
what is the one thing
that Arithmetic never does?"
In one sure voice they answer:

Unlike our sinful selves,
sums and debits never lie.

HOW HARD I TRY
Lucy Annie Smith, Rock Creek Road, Snake River Country, 1889

Missus, the lawyer says
I need a witness.
Cruelty the grounds and I want
custody of my infants.
Frank is merciless
to me, our children, the livestock,
at times maniacal especially
when fueled by drink. Never speaks
a pleasant word, either he snaps my head off
or pays no attention, though
I have run afoot to help him
corral stock, trap gophers, prairie dogs,
burn and grub brush, all when I felt sick
enough to be abed. Our quarter section
just as much mine as his.
I have taken in wash, boarders, anything
to earn a penny to feed us. Frank
always takes the money,
says he'll have me put in prison
for stealing it back. When the baby
screamed for a week, I told him
I had to take her to the dentist.
He called me vile names,
drew his fist back, then let
twenty-five head of livestock starve
rather than sell them to buy
medicine for infant gum complaint.

You're the schoolteacher
and have no doubt heard
the neighbors speak of his mania
for throwing things in the river
—coal oil cans, saddle
blankets, all sorts of filth—we
have to drink that water.

He is vulgar before the children;
education, he says, will make them fools;
tells them he'll be glad
when they're gone or dead, then he'll not
have to milk or keep a cow.

I cannot please him
though I've made over old clothes; patched
and worn skirts as long as they can be made
to hold together. He rages
when I sell a few eggs.
His brother begs us to visit, but
Frank says I am not good enough to go,
though I am good enough to mend the glass
when the window's broken, good enough
to seal the walls with old boxes torn to bits.
I had to get up too soon
after the children were born to help
him nurse the calves. Right after
we married, he started burning
my cattle with his brand.
Missus, I need a witness
before he sells the last heifer
that has my *rocking A* on her shoulder.
When the buyer comes for the cattle next week,
shall I tell him I want the money
for that cow? The children have no winter
underclothes. Even before this sick spell
I felt run down. You would not
know about the value of his
four hundred horses and six hundred beef, but

Remember when he nailed the schoolyard
gate shut so that everyone had to
climb the fence? I do not know who else
I can call to be my witness. He never
takes a bath, won't even wash
his hands after milking and goes to bed
wearing his dirtiest shirt.

He nailed the schoolyard gate shut,
but leaves our gate open;
I have to watch my children every minute
for fear of their falling in the river.
He fights with his help,
his neighbors. He told your husband
that he cannot keep whiskey
in our house for fear I'll drink it.
When he drove the stock to Omaha,
I had to borrow from the hired man
to buy a ham. Frank found out,
struck me on the head till I thought
my eardrum broken.

When I had nineteen teeth
drawn out, he made me ride home
in a lumber wagon without dinner
and later slammed doors so that
my head might split. He burns my mail,
puts his manurey boots on the table,
soiling every school book
you gave the children.
My lawyer, a friend of Frank's,
wants a hundred dollars.
Don't you think Frank
should be the one to pay?
I could tell enough mean things
to fill a ledger, but guess
this will do for now. I am well
worked up over these proceedings
—cannot eat or sleep.
If I don't quit, I'll talk myself hoarse and
tomorrow be unfit to plead my case.
The sitting judge is a friend of Frank's.
If anyone could help me through this,
it would be you.

COMES NOW SAID DEFENDANT
Frank Smith, Rock Creek Road,
Snake River Country, 1889

Of course I deny it, though admit
I married Annie and wrought two children.
That she has always conducted
and deported herself as a true
affectionate faithful wife, I categorically
and under oath deny.
I deny any guilt of extreme cruelty
or any cruelty at all. Never
did I offer her such indignities
as to render her condition intolerable.
I deny that I refused her sufficient
means to clothe herself;
I deny that times without number I failed
to provide the children with meat necessary
for sustenance; I deny that I refused
to supply needed medical attention; I deny
I abused her or ever called her vile names.
I deny that I possess an ungovernable temper.
When did I ever take one sip of whiskey?
I deny that in the autumn of last year
I struck and slapped her about the head.
I deny falsely accusing her of stealing
money, my writing desk, or wash machine.
I deny that she was compelled to leave
her home, deny that I ordered her *leave*,
deny that I told her never to set foot therein again;
deny that I am not a fit person to have
custody of my beloved children.

I am hard working and without capital,
except for a small sage ranch worth nothing.
I deny I have six hundred head of cattle or
any cattle at all. I admit
to owning a few horses, broncs
and old mares without value.

I admit she's of querulous and malicious
disposition, but deny that things cannot
be patched up between us; I deny
that she is in feeble health
unable to support herself;
I deny that her sole property
is a twenty dollar cow and that she is dependent
upon her relatives; I deny
that thirty dollars per annum a reasonable sum
for her support and adamantly deny
that one hundred dollars
a reasonable attorney's fee.
I have always supplied her generously
considering my means;
clothed, fed, doctored her despite
her constant bickering, fault-finding
and systematic endeavors to tantalize me
into giving her some shadow
of a ground for maltreatment
and therefore enticing me
into litigation
and stealing my ranch.

Didn't I willingly give her
opportunities for making money:
keeping chickens, cows, running
a stage stop, all done at my expense?
She has always tried to make trouble
and without cause deserted
my home wrongfully taking
our infants, nearly stripping the house and
to date not returned, but instead thrown herself
and the tiny children for whom she cannot provide
upon the mercy of the tax payers of this town.
I ask you,

What could this woman be thinking?

SWANS, A LETTER NOT SENT
Frances Stanton, Cottonwood, Idaho, 1889

Is it the loneliness of this place or
the unceasing wind
that has brought me to madness?
I, who never fancied my husband,
fancy strangers. You, for instance.
"How long can it blow without
respite?" you asked.
"Five days? Two weeks?"

The night before we met, I dreamt
the swans who desert me each May
stayed on, but refused to speak.
Mockingbirds in lower willow rungs
went mute while magpies flagged their tails
at a white mane of wings.
Cobra-headed and brass-beaked,
each pair ruled Mint Lake inlets
by arrogance, symmetry and
mysterious lion-clawed, iron-colored feet.

In my dream, I asked after
their ugly young. Hose-necked bundles
of mustard flower and tar,
the white goddesses had hidden
their currency away
in haystack rocks off shore, safe,
guarded by white magnificent necks
and black magnificent feet. On the beach,
mockingbirds stole wolf howl and snake hiss,
hammered out lyrics as magpie tails
flagged the iambic clomp-
clomp of a saddle horse's beat. But
pyrite eyes only blinked,
floated on;
the Order of Aphrodite wanted no song.

I awoke, feeling empty of everything
except fatigue. The razor wind still cut
what grass grew between scab
rocks and a heat snake mirage of lake.
On the stage road, the snap of gravel
against iron shoe—the sorrowful tempo
of a lone horseman's trot.

You rode past with matted grass-
clumped hair pale as dust; the air filled
with the raw smell of just-tanned leather
and sweat. Your horse caught my eye—color
of a grindstone, silhouette of a swan.

THE INCLEMENT WEATHER
OF THE HEART
Frances Stanton, Cottonwood, Idaho, 1889

Standing river edge, barefoot
on duck egg stones, this
my secret place.
I study the cool white
light of mirrored stars
floating in night ink
and drink the thin
blue milk of your face.
If only the bright
kerosene lanterns
of my insomnia
could fuel my days where
the anchor of your smile
has let me drift into the Snake's
violent water. No child
of Luna, the moons
of Jupiter have their fix on you.

Mutiny, mutiny, Reason screams,
but repeatedly I grab
and claw for the hooks
of your mouth, though
your surly stare batters
my chest and I am sucked
into a whirlpool vortex where
water forces its way through
my mouth, backward into lungs.
I choke. How long
will the lifeless broth of you
be the only sustenance my

soul craves? Ghost
lights of river stars
bob at my feet,
giving no warmth.
I connect them like dots
into an outline of your face.
There is no accounting for
the quivering arc of your smile.
There is no accounting for
the inclement weather of the heart.

BORROWED HORSES
Duke Deneke, Open Range Country,
Idaho/Wyoming, 1889

What shepherd having a hundred does not leave the
ninety-nine and go after the one that is lost?

i.
Jesus Never Owned a Horse

Father owned three thousand sheep
and a colt I coveted above all else.
Hiding from the odor of wool, I watched
pinking sunsets, and dreamed
it a weaned grown stallion.
I loved best (next to the horse) firearms,
making toy pistols—most taken away.
On my imaginary horse I galloped
shooting snakes, buzzards, porcupines, anything
to contrive the smell of powdered lead.
Tough as sole leather, I'd sleep
—regardless of weather—in sage
with only sweaty saddle blankets for cover.
Finally, I asked father for the horse.
He gave—a wonder.
I collected toy guns faster
than they could be destroyed and with them
vexed and confounded the sheep,
their fat flat bobbed tails
my favorite target. At school,
teacher pronounced me unruly,
promising all kinds of punishment—
a hemp necktie attached to a tree, for one.
I developed an instinct peculiar to wolves:
watching the multitudes unseen.
When my bronc was old enough to saddle,
father turned the horse over to another boy
and later sold it to him.

Unlimbering my trigger
temper, I struck out
on my own across the rangeland.
Though only fourteen, got a job
shoveling coal for the railroad,
but forfeited it. Got a job
driving dowgies, lost it—always taking
severance pay in horseflesh. Captured
every range bronc I could rope,
branded or unbranded
—wasn't I handy with fire poker
and ear notching knife? My character
plain as print, some said;
though not my father's sheep
whose company I began to seek when hiding,
running my hands over their flat backs,
grasping clumps of fetid greasy fur, consoled
by their bleating litany which never
knew the snake-hiss word,
horsethief.

ii
**Rules to Know When
Moveable and Immoveable Feasts Begin**

At the Feast of All Souls, our herd split
into scores and scattered
beneath basalt ledges
sheltering sandstone caves
and handfuls of frost-killed grass.
Bucks put with ewes at Christmas.
By Twelfth Night—the worst of the blizzards—
five months minus five days until lambing.
Palm Sunday, we mounted up,
trailing sheep from winter range
to lambing ground to summer pasture.
In drifting snow, traveled by dead
reckoning and the second rule

of sheep husbandry:
bring thy flocks daily to water.
To turn the herd, asked the dogs to speak
in high voices. Sheep
so easily befuddled. Not to run,
I told them, not to miss
one bite of grass.

The first rule: Protect.
The three dangers: beasts, theft,
the weather. We lived nearby
in white canvas-walled tents banked with dirt
keeping out the snow—or shelters made
of rock slabs the color of bacon.
Possessions: dog, borrowed horse,
a small woodstove, and a routine
varied by season and moon phase.

Wool sheared just after Easter.
Though scissoring fleece caused no pain,
the bleaters feared for their lives,
hurtling suicidally in any direction.
Lambs born before Ascension.
When ewes neared labor
leaving the herd, we re-stacked
stone folds—cold spring rain
death to a newborn.
After lambing, brought together
the multitudes, docking tails. Careful
the dogs didn't wear their paw pads off
in the gathering of flocks.
If lamb sales paid expenses,
then gunny bags of wool, our profit;
prices for winter hay determining
if our mounts kept or turned loose.

iii
Astride, the Soldiers of Herod Flew Without Wings

The night before we were to drive
our flock to market train, frost
turned the aspen orange among black
pines and pricked the seed pods
of vine rose crimson as our Savior's wounds.
The fattened herd bedded down
on the first grass grown up in a burn
brought on by lightning.
When stars still fluttered
weakly in heaven's vault,
six barrel-chested strangers came asking
for the flock master, my father.
Others lurked in the lean-legged trees.
An odor whispered, *cattlemen;*
whispered, *freshly oiled artillery.*
I had no doubt it was me they wanted.
A sheriff? Or the quick and sure
Vigilance Committee? (My borrowed horses
pastured just one gulch away.)
When father came forward, they bound
his wrists behind him, pulled
a noose over his head, securing
the rope's end around the corral's top rail.
Another pushed me to the ground as I tried
to explain, then with bootheel broke
our wagon's wheels using spokes as clubs.
(Where were their guns?)
Shouting, *It's me you want*, I got stung
across the nose with a quirt for my trouble.
They pulled father up by the neck
six inches off the ground. I could feel
his muscles clench and skin redden as they
extracted a promise. Then I heard
their artillery, saw their multitudes stalk
down from the trees like wolves, and knew
why they'd saved their ammunition.

The sheep, frantic, shrieked like infants.
The price on my head no connection
to these bloody doings. In less time than
the lightning lash that caused
the forest fire they blamed us for,
guns exploded into the smell
of saltpeter, raw whiskey, and sweat;
our three thousand slain to a battle cry
that fires forever every sleepless night since.
I thought of my lambs bleeding to death,
orphans I had nursed,
building sage fires to warm them
against a world blasted by hail.

The Vigilance Committee departed
as swiftly as they had struck,
leaving us awaiting a slow
uncertain courthouse justice.
Like the horses
I would have to turn loose
because I could not buy hay to feed them,
(unless
I was caught, tried, found guilty of theft
and sent to the penitentiary) we were all

winterkill now.

THAT SPRINGTIME OF HER LIFE
Frances Stanton, Cottonwood, Idaho, 1890

Smell of cold clay, abalone shell sky, a drumroll of wind
and soon my hair studded with waterpox. Bad storm, no
safe place, no one sees it. Just the cat and myself on the
porch, sewing in hand. In the west, clouds like cauliflowers
bloom through a tear of sky. I want to rip off my flesh all
those mule years, down to young bones, erasing the
parenthesis that fixes my mouth. If I had God's paint brush
for just one hour, I'd fix the rat-brown landscape and—
closer to the water—the fountains of gnats. If I squint,
willow bud near the glass arrow of river bursts into cherry.
A mutter of mallard wings, whisper of feet behind me, the
laugh of a dog. Noises of hammering. A heart. See the rare
geometry of his vanished face in a stranger's, in a hump of
rock, in any man who walks twisted out of true. His taste
in the air, his tongue rough as the cat's, his rain smell. My
lips slippery with butter: On the porch sewing: *School mam,
school mam, well-corseted, well-shod, never leaves her house
without a bonnet on.* My greatest passion, it has been said,
tatting lace doilies into lengthening days, months of lunar
halos. No one sees the bad storm, the no safe crossing,
waters the color of creosote, rain stabbing everything like
nettles. The noise of hammering again—a heart, a heart.
Run my needle through it.

TWO FOR A PENNY,
COUNTING MY RAT-HUNTING MONEY
Mary Hannah Clark, age 14, Cottonwood,
Idaho, 1890

Late night: a carriage wreck of pots
below me in the kitchen.
In the morning, blood
marks the laundry tub where Mama
skewered a rat with a fork
—that's one less for me.

When Mama takes in Miss Teacher's wash,
I study each shirring, ruffle, pinking; turn
every dress inside out examining the details:
how lined, bound, how even and small
each stitch, every dart and seam—seventeen
to a silk basque. Look here, Mama says,
this lining so pieced and patched. Pity
your teacher, taken in by her dressmaker.

I think it beautiful, beg to be let iron it.
How I sweat, trying to get it shiny
without the scorch. My gaze transfixed
in what mama calls my Satan-
filled bedroomy eyes.
When the sadiron sticks, I run
it over salt, then a candle only to get
more wrinkles in than out.

Teacher has three smocks, boots
laced up to her knees. My clothes
made from gunny bags and ore satchels;
my bustle, dish towels folded over
an empty peach tin strung through
and tied round my waist with a string.
And these underthings? Cut
from sugar sacks, the word *sugar*
stamped in the most peculiar places.

After I told Father, I wanted
to be a school marm—wearing
real underwear and swishing skirts—
he said, Talk like that, sister,
no more schooling for you. He muttered
something about fast women, whetted
his sawyer's ragged-toothed blade.

For bangles, I bored holes in a handful
of pennies—my rat-hunting money—ready
to sew them on my cashmere shawl
should I be presented with one. I want
tight fitting waists, circular satin flounces;
a Chinese fan, the first thing I'll buy.
I've made a list. Then a burgundy sash
of watered ribbon, never again a rope belt.
Mornings I'll dress in lace scrims,
black velvet band at my throat.

At school, they laugh at my torn undershirt,
the socks I wear as mittens. Today
I feign illness; wait until father leaves for the mill,
then mend Miss Teacher's hem bound in thin
satin braid that I rub between thumb
and forefinger. The comfort
of exquisite fabric protected
on cold days by teacher's green wool cape
with little fur heads for fasteners.

My list,
my Marshal Field catalogue cutouts
of women in Alsatian bows,
my collection of fabric (a square
of real linen from a man's white shirt)
secreted in a rat hole beneath my mattress.
At night, stroking my linen swatch,
I stare into space
staggered by elegance, then fall to sleep
dreaming the worst—not that the rat

used my treasures for nesting, but
that I'm caught: Mama sobs.
Holding hard the reins
of my fast women traits,
father yanks me from school
—*teaching daughters to read*
only hastens disgrace.

Waking in sweat, I count sheep, blessings,
rats scurrying across the floor.
I'm too breathless for sleep.

I HAVE ALWAYS BELIEVED IT IS ENTIRELY POSSIBLE TO PRAY WHILE CHOPPING WOOD

To: Mrs. Frances Stanton, Cottonwood School, Snake River Country, 1890

Dear Missus,

Your letter in hand, I do not regret my decision and am thankful to hear that all four of my children have stopped trembling like aspen when called upon to recite. I apologize for them having tried your patience. Some say life is patterned at birth and cannot be re-stitched. Coming into this country from Wales as a bride, I crossed Clear Creek with one horse that spooked, kicking the end-gate out of the wagon box. My trunk with every keepsake, bolt of cloth, photograph, lace, button, book I owned slid off the back, never heard of again.

How often since that day have I had to start again from scratch? Sam, the children's father, had gone to Onion Gulch delivering a team, came home riding a little Indian digger bareback. He'd lost everything on a bet: wagons, money for clothes for the children, and cloth to make real pretty curtains for our dugout's window. My lost trunk again...oh, how it might have saved me. We separated. I traded a horse I found on the range for wood, took in wash, traded garden truck for a thousand pounds of Snow Flake brand flour that became the pride of my heart. Bought a glass window, making curtains from one of the flour sacks. Always more uses for sacking than sacks— underwear, table linens, diapers, dyed pieces for a quilt— wouldn't you agree? Daily I walked around the flour piled in the center of the floor like a cattle king surveying his stock. For Christmas, I polished my window, filled the dishpan with popcorn, and from potatoes and corncobs made rag dolls, black beans for eyes. I could not help but weep over our plenty: a tree decorated with trinkets the children had saved: wishbones of wild ducks, stars cut from rabbit pelts, foil from tea boxes. Suspended by thread, each star danced in the wee disturbances of air—the door opening or the stove heating up. After New Years, I got the

P.O. contract, had a little store and ran a peddler's wagon up, down the river during round-up time selling such things as cowboys need—tobacco, Arbuckle's coffee, Watkins black sage potion. Come August, the range grass burned up, blew away. Another winter stared me in the face.

Sam swore he'd reformed. I took him back. By November, the cattle looked like hides thrown over so many junipers. They ate quilts I pinned on the line, gnawed creek willows to stumps, during a bad storm when they banked up against the house, broke my window. Sam came home late, shooting holes in the sky, barely able to walk. I didn't have to pack, he'd gambled away even the flour. Leaving in a borrowed wagon, the children and I lived like beasts, often taking refuge in a bear den. My greatest worry, sickness. My most terrifying moment when I had to pour coal oil down Bessie's croupy throat to get her to breathe. For two years we wandered—outcasts, sleeping, eating (July heat or winter blizzard) under the wagon. Taken in by Indians, painted ladies, men whose history it was unwise to question. I do not regret my decision, but how often did I hold head in hands, thinking: If only I had my trunk, the better citizens wouldn't look at us like coyotes.

Finally I got us a place—walls unchinked so rats came through the logs, but with a doorknob instead of a latchstring. My first correspondence received here: word of Sam's death. As you know, months passed before the children grew accustomed to civilized life and did not run away hiding like animals or speak in tongues of the Shoshones whose bear den we lived in. Again, I apologize for their behavior trying your soul. Trusting everything to you, do with them what you think best and in your prayers, ask God to look down on this manless house and smile.

Remaining in Your Debt, Martha James.

I DRIVE YOU FROM MY HEART
Frances Stanton, Snake River Crossing
Cottonwood, Idaho, 1890

With thorn bushes,
with a flailing razor strop,
I drive you from my heart,
throw rocks at you,
throw gravel shards
at your two burnt matchstick
eyelid slits. The black
coachwhip snake
of your smile I hatchet
with a dull carving knife;
with the sharpest pick
pummel your bloodless cyanide
peach pit heart. With knitting
needles, nails, I drive you
from every cell of memory.
I stab slivers through
the bridge of your nose,
your brow's overhang,
then hammer down
your high-peaked cheek bones.
From my body I purge
you like the crabs
of cancer, like heavy
affliction of the lungs, like
misery in my joints.
I drive you, drive you
from my heart.

Scarecrow, scarecrow,
I infect the straws of you
with scorpions. Armies

of stinging ants march you
from my thoughts. Your silent
secretive glacial soul I drive
away from me. Your once seraph
face turns to cabbage,
a common worm-eaten
scalped head-of-a-cabbage.
I bruise your ears
with gun powder screams.
I drive you, drive you out.

I see you sleeping under houses,
see your scarred dog face snarling up.
I put the feral dog you are
in a river skiff come unmoored
in an ice floe when flood waters
hide the rocks, watch you trudge
to shore, legs bleeding as you
labor through hip-deep snow,
face shining with hoarfrost.
I hold furnace slag
to the frayed seams
of the clothes I made for you,
to the rags that are your hair.
The pitiful fire you become
empties my heart of you.
I throw your bones into the rain-
soaked street, make you
no different than mud, throw
your ashes to the Nor'easters so
no part of you will have another
for companionship. My hands,
arms, my clothes covered
with grit, the soot of you
thick on me.

When I am bathed
and empty of you, I sweep
you into the corner
of an unheated room,
bury tintypes of you
in a trunk under the bed where
your onyx eyes pale
from mold never again
to glare at me as if to spit.
With your face
driven into history, I finally,
finally free the river
of the mire of you,

and cross over.

SIXTH GRADE COMPOSITION:
WHY WE CAME HERE
Jarvis Fisher, Cottonwood School House, 1890

My new teacher says the weather's tow
sack of grief is no answer to this, though
three perished. One child's body
not found until a March thaw.
To fully know the blizzard,
you have to understand the day before—how
a southerly wind reshaped the drifts and
the Nebraska sky seared the deep
blue of our scarcity of coal. At dusk
the sun turned the color of anger.
Gales that night, but by daybreak low slung
dead calm clouds made the cow fussy
at milking. Walking to school,
so warm the snow verged
on melting—sheer joy after three
storm-heavy months. As the church
bell chimed ten, just as we'd set
our spelling books aside, like a bat
against a wall, hard flakes rammed
the schoolhouse. Every object blotted out:
the red hand sled just outside the door,
teacher's house twenty paces away,
the catalpa tree we climbed at recess.
As mice ran across our feet to escape
the awful roaring, teacher kept us
reading Homer. The building shook.
Dismissed, we glutted around
the hot stove, not enough coal to last
the night. A child could live only a short time
lost in a storm like this—what best to do?
Take hands, said Teacher:
small child, large child, don't anyone dare
let go—nothing can save you.
Teacher at the north end,
smallest student in the middle; largest, I was

therefore last in line. Keep a sharp lookout
for the house: miss it, we perish.
My job: to count steps.
Ready, one, two; the smaller ones gasped
as we hit the gale. Teacher kept talking,
encouraging, twice calling: *still there?*
Our line unbroken as we walked into solid
whiteness, the going not so bad
where we quartered the wind.
Teacher called for the number of steps.
No house. Turn north? South?
The church bell's muted tinning our only beacon.
Something struck my foot, a box elder,
the house threshold but a few feet away,
though we did not see it until I fell,
nearly knocking my forehead on it.
When we opened the door, rats ran in before us.
The first thing Teacher did, a count of scholars.
We slept on the floor, at midnight the wind lulled,
by morning only a stiff breeze, two sun dogs and
all day snow ran over the drifts like pollen.
At another town school, a teacher
had locked the students in, burning desks then
the floor for heat. Three perished:
a man who went out to tend his cow, a boy
coming late to class who fell face down, and
the schoolteacher my father was betrothed to.
When none of father's fiancée's pupils came
she tried to return to her boarding place.
Next day people launched a search.
When a family who'd gone to bed
to save fuel and provisions got up
to feed their chickens, they heard
their haystack moan. She'd dug
her way in, though not far enough,
one leg frozen to the thigh.
My own father rushed her to the doctor
fast as possible on such terrible roads.
The limb amputated.

She lived for a week. If you were
all the time looking for the coal train
through a telescope, you could see
her boarding house from ours.

Thesis, evidence, conclusion.
My new teacher asks, What
is the purpose of my composition?
The wanderings of real life, unlike
the wanderings of Odysseus, lack
a unity necessary to essay examination.
She asks me, *What about* why
you came here from Nebraska?

ANTE-OVER THE OUTSIDE BISSY
Annabelle Nelson, Age 11
Cottonwood School House, 1890

No girl dared go during recess, so we played ante-over
the outside bissy—though we'd no ball, but made a
beanbag and put corn in it. Big Boy Mikey McGregor
bored a hole in back of the six-seat bissy and made a sign
when a girl would come. Big had no mercy, so fat he had
bosoms. Fifteen, even little Cassie read better than him.
Boys pelted rocks at the wall, peeked through knotholes,
opened the outhouse door, throwing fresh horse apples in.

Big liked to corner me and kiss me, telling everyone I
tasted like soap. He stank of silage, had brown rings on his
hands from morning milking. Big never washed and the
stench of cow stayed on me, made me not want to eat my
lunch. Sometimes we girls had funerals for the prairie dogs
he killed. With Miss Teacher's dress starched so stiff, you
could hear her come up behind you, so Big McGregor
never got caught. He caused teacher's neck to turn red as
turkey wattles by constantly moving the desk we shared.
After Miss Teacher spiked it to the floor, he put a snake in
her recitation box.

During class, raise two fingers, and teacher excused you
to go the outside bissy. During recess, Big Mike tormented
any girl who went in there. When we played ante-over the
outhouse, sometimes one of us could sneak in. Once our
beanbag got caught on the roof. We lifted little Cassie up to
get it down, which is how and why she knew another
thing the boys would do: wet the bissy's back wall with
their tools. How far up could they mark, a contest. Cassie
told me: Big Mikey knew how to squirt and won. I told
teacher everything: the kissing, the telling everyone I
smelled like soap, those brown rings on his fingers from
milking, the tool-wetting contest on the bissy's back wall
and how Big Mickey won. Miss Teacher took a ruler to my
hands and arms and head, bloodying my nose. But, that
afternoon Miss Teacher wrote a note home to Big
McGregor's mother: *as a matter of hygiene, please, after barn
chores, get his hands washed up a little bit cleaner.*

WE NEVER SPEAK OF IT
Frances Stanton, Cottonwood, 1890

When the schoolhouse's flagstone step
went missing, we knew exactly what
became of it. Diphtheria season over,
a different sore throat, perhaps
scarlet fever's sharp scythe, cut
across our threshold, no one knew precisely.
The price of everything soaring, so
no doctor called, no one to caution
about a weakening heart.

How many times have I put paper
and ink at his desk, searched
for his coat in the cloakroom?
Hearing thunder, I've looked out
to a muddy game of Red Rover,
all scholars accounted for, except
the smallest boy... Then I'd
remember how he always arrived at school
late, swinging his dinner pail,
an old lard bucket, a red pig painted on it,
his initials punched into the lid.

I took dried baby's breath tied
with white ribbon to his mother.
The worst, his birthday when
Annabelle, Cassie, Claire asked where
I thought he'd gone to. We drew pictures
of his favorite things: molasses men,
a mountain of mashed potatoes with clouds
of butter sunshining down the slopes. Sometimes,
out my side vision, I think I see him
up to vexing tricks, stuffing gunnysacks
up the stove pipe. How many times
did I lace his legs with a switch?

First of May brought warmer winds,
most children no longer wore
all their clothes at once.
During recess before the end-
of-the-year Spelling Bee, Cassie
and the younger ones shouted:
A miracle, come see. Sure it's some excuse—
they'd not studied their word lists—
still, I let them pull me along, stumbling
on the missing step, stifling curse words,
past where Jim Hill's men surveyed
for track and trestle. We played How Many:
new tents like mushrooms, foot deep
ruts in the road, fresh white-faced calves,
how many pickets missing from the fence
around it, how many columns of unpainted
wooden crosses. Then my eye ran
to a lap robe of green and burst of white,
the baby's breath bouquet
filled with seed pods had ignited
around a familiar stepping stone
turned upright now amid a pile of rocks.
On it inscribed in capital letters, the name
chiseled into all our hearts, *ARTHUR,*
5 years, 11 months, 29 days.

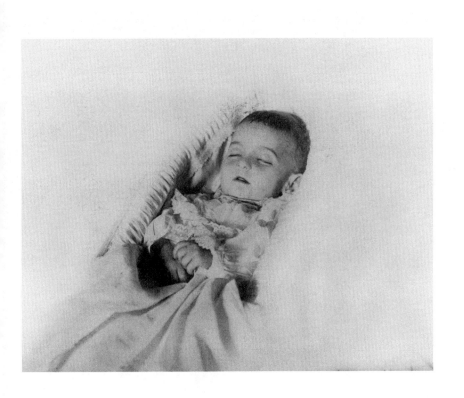

AFTERWORD

In 1993, I published a book of linked dramatic monologues, *Oh How Can I Keep on Singing?*, poems based on the lives of women and children who immigrated to the Okanogan Valley in north central Washington State during the later half of the Nineteenth Century. I had not set out to write this book, but fell into it by happy accident. Living on a farm in the Northwest, I sought common ground and inspiration from my rural foremothers: how did they cope with isolation, with a life dependent on the vagaries of the weather and the eternal gray sweep of sky? What, in newborn livestock, accounts for the incredible urge for or the total lack of what is often called "willingness to thrive"? Uncovering reminiscences collected by the *Okanogan Independent* in the 1920s led to my discovering further reminiscences by some of the same players collected by a branch of the Works Project Administration, the Federal Writers' Project, a decade later. These readings led to visits to historical archives, which led to meetings and interviews with the descendants of the pioneers, which led to conversations with the pioneers' children still alive at the time, some aged into the 100s. Speaking with these descendants opened a Christmas stocking of lost minutiae: *Would I like to see Dad's branding iron? Would I like to see the mortar and pestle Mother played at Saturday night socials? Would I like to hear about the intricacies of playing the comb and washboard? Would I like to read Grandma's cookbook—her recipe for pitcher plant tea, a good cancer medication?* One treads on hallowed ground when one writes about someone else's dearly departed, and so I published the book with much trepidation. In the meantime, Moving Images Video made a film for educational television based on these poems. Its Okanogan début took place in the town of Molson, population thirty-five. Two-hundred and fifty people attended and were served a home-cooked dinner made from local beef, tomatoes, corn, apples, etc. Now the book and the making of this film have become part of their historical archives.

In the meantime, I found myself preoccupied with the lives of Northwest pioneer women and children. I could not stop writing about them, and published another book of poems, *The Dust of Everyday Life*, as well as a novel, *The Pearl of Ruby City*, on the same subject. During these endeavors one fact began to cast a mournful eye at me: all the reminiscences, diaries, and interviews I'd studied (pored over, re-read, underlined, memorized) belonged to a select community, i.e., those who had made it to the Pacific Ocean, to Oregon or Washington Territory or to Vancouver, British Columbia, and the gold fields of the Kootenay. They or their parents belonged to that seemingly fortunate group that had arrived at their planned destination, or near to it—that group that had come all the way along the Oregon or Overland Trail. What about the people, particularly the women and children, who either by accident or design didn't travel all the way to the coast? What about the immigrants who got stranded, who got marooned or ran out of money, whose wagons broke, husbands died or oxen perished? What about the immigrants who ended up living along the trail? So much of my own life—like the writing of *Oh How Can I Keep on Singing?*—had happened by accident, that I couldn't help but wonder about these settlers' sudden change of plans, their accidental relocation to Idaho, Utah, or Wyoming. I began to stalk historical archives, both public and private, for news of this latter community.

My obsessive search took me to Laramie for six months where I worked as Visiting Writer at the University of Wyoming. Here on the Continental Divide, my viewpoint of the West forever changed. Having been born in California, I'd spent most of my adult life in the Bay Area and Seattle or in the mid-Atlantic, which is to say that I had little experience of life in the U.S. other than residing on one seaboard or the other. Soon after my arrival in Laramie, it became clear to me that Wyoming-ites saw LA-SF-Seattle as the West *Coast,* Boston-New York-DC as the East *Coast,* and themselves and the high plains as *True* West. Less than half a million people live in this state of few trees, arctic winters, rocks like lunar landscapes, and Pleistocene ice. Outsiders are suspect—they arrive, reap the profits (from mineral and natural gas deposits, livestock, dinosaur fossils, etc.), then depart. Some of my undergraduate students' parents (born in the 1950s) remembered life before indoor plumbing and as children had been lulled to sleep at night to the music of creek water flowing outside their doors. When their ranch houses got indoor toilets, the noise of the pipes kept them awake into the wee hours. Giving poetry-writing workshops across the state, I drove for hours on two-lane highways over what looked like arctic tundra often passing no houses and maybe one car. In a few almost sacred places, teepee rings and wagon wheel ruts were still visible. Truly I had found a door to the Nineteenth Century American frontier. On one memorable journey in early spring, I left Laramie on a Friday and drove through a blizzard for countless unsettling hours on a narrow highway to the petroleum tank-dotted hills of Casper. On my return the following Sunday afternoon, not only had all the snow melted, but the now cloudless sky had turned a Caribbean blue and the treeless brown hills were dappled in a very pale green. As I rounded a bend in the lonely road, there before me bloomed a field of what had to be a thousand white ewes grazing with their few-days-old lambs.

At the American Heritage archives in Laramie, the Wyoming State archives in Cheyenne, the Idaho State Historical Society in Boise, and the archives of Washington State University in Pullman, I read letters, testimonials, reminiscences, and diaries of people who had come to *True* West following dreams, cavalry officers, mining booms, railroad work, livestock and stage-stop ventures. I also found documentation of those who indeed had broken down or run out of money along their way to the Pacific and had literally settled where the oxen died. Some reminiscences leapt out at me because of their comic relief. Consider the first pineapple served in Moscow, Idaho. No one had seen anything like the spiny-looking gourd and so a schoolteacher-librarian had to be consulted as to how to "attack" the frightful looking thing. On a more serious note, I may never cease to reflect on the sobering tale of Martha James, a lady's maid who traveled to Wyoming from Wales in the employ of a titled Englishwoman. Martha married a ranch hand, homesteaded and then, after losing everything several times due to her husband's drunkenness and compulsive gambling, wandered for two years through western Wyoming. In bad weather (which must have been unimaginable considering the severity of winters in the Big Horn Mountains), she cared for and schooled her five youngsters in caves and under her peddler's wagon. Lesson one, she taught her children, was that they had a lot to be proud of: no one in their family had ever been divorced, arrested, or failed to pay his own way.

Because I am a teacher, I began to see things through the eyes of a frontier schoolmarm. Many of the authors of the archival documents I read had attended as students or had labored as teachers in one-room schools. In addition to being saddled with the responsibility of rendering the young literate, frontier teachers were also sometimes called upon to perform the duties of custodian, nurse, dentist, social worker, child advocate, counselor, lawyer, letter-writer, translator, psychologist, and mediator. Often she—territorial teachers were predominately female—was as young as eighteen and it was not uncommon that some of her male students were older and taller than she was. I read heart-felt testimonies of pillars-of-the-community whose childhood home life had been in unspeakable disarray and whose teacher had saved him/her from an untoward fate. Likewise occasional senators, governors, captains of industry professed that they would never have gone further than the third grade if it had not been for the kindness and understanding of Miss/Mrs./Mr. Such-and-such. Frontier teachers were paid a pittance with women receiving even less compensation than their male counterparts; a male teacher would have to be offered a wage competitive with clerical work (generally not open to women), a salary not affordable by fledgling school districts. In addition to cleaning the school before and after class and chopping the wood to heat it, a frontier teacher taught all grades in one room, the older students helping the younger and everyone rocking the teacher's baby who, for reasons touched upon in a moment, might have been counted as a student rather than a dependant. If it was even rumored that a female teacher had married, she was relieved of her duties immediately. Predictably a married woman would become pregnant and it was considered inappropriate for a visibly pregnant woman to be seen in public, particularly where her changing physiology could be scrutinized by impressionable young minds. Older schoolmarms usually taught in teacher's colleges, called "normal schools" or, in the event of a lack of qualified males, served as superintendents.

However, in boom towns and mining camps and railroad ports-of-call on the waterless sage sea of *True* West, trained educators were few and compensation almost non-existent. Thus communities made do with the talent they had on hand: sometimes the oldest pupil stood in as teacher or sometimes it was a young married woman—baby in tow—or an untrained but mature lady who happened to be the wife of, say, the mining company's visiting geologist. An individual such as this latter matron—usually newly arrived in this outpost of progress—finding herself with time on her hands, was accustomed to the civic duties and good works incumbent upon a woman of her social position. Her previous teaching experience, if any, might have been in a Sunday school. Discipline problems, the learning disabled, those with speech impediments and vision deficiencies, the non-English-speaking, the infirm, the hungry and ill-clothed, the emotionally and psychologically traumatized, all landed in her lap in classes possibly as large as sixty pupils. Often a teacher tied her more recalcitrant students to a chair. The debate wasn't to tie or not to tie, but how best to tie. One northern Minnesota teacher, fearing that a certain fidgety boy would run out of the school room into a nearby lake and drown, tied him down. That exact tragedy occurred on the next teacher's watch when the new instructor failed to adequately secure him to his chair.

The idea of producing a sequel to *Oh How Can I Keep on Singing?*, a collection of poems concerning the actual residents of an actual valley, felt daunting given the lucky heart-warming reception of those monologues. And so as I continued to be haunted by this community of people who by design or accident had settled *True* West, I began to imagine a composite-of-a-place near the Idaho-Wyoming border. I began to think of the voices of the reminiscences I had read as the residents of the environs of this mythical town and further visualized this region from this outsider's, this mature middle-class teacher's point of view. She would be a woman with problems of her own, displaced, with no friends of her ilk. I considered the oddity of her from the point of view of her pupils.

I called this imagined town Cottonwood after that one stout, tall but shallow-rooted and therefore volatile tree on the frying-pan flat horizon; a tree symbolic of water, of relief from the sun, a tree which promised wood for fuel, leaves for animal feed, cotton for batting, branches for roof thatch, and shelter from a June deluge. I imagined the people whose reminiscences I read living in or nearby the mythical Cottonwood (not to be confused with the actual town of that name) which I placed near the Snake River, or on their way to or from this stage-stop-of-a-place in the year 1889 when, because of the previous devastating winter, the consolidation of the railroad in some places and its expansion in others, because of labor unrest and the uncertain financial times, many found themselves on the move to they-knew-not-where.

This teacher: I began to imagine her correspondence: letters from and news of students who had left school to marry, to work in the mines, to serve out sentences for—to pick one of the most common crimes of the day—horse theft in state and local prisons some of which were privatized. School children have such a keen sense of justice, of what is fair and unfair, so I pondered also the psychological effects of the vast number of pupils harvested from the classroom each year by those now forgotten outlaws: diphtheria, tetanus, polio, malaria, whooping cough, cholera, dysentery, and typhoid, to name a few.

In doing this pondering, the idea of the *outlaw* stayed with me, possibly because some percentage of those who came west in this era did not come just to better their lives, but to escape legal, moral, or social authority. Possibly also the idea of the outlaw stayed with me because my farm is located near a town populated by four prisons and because I once, quite by chance, taught a workshop in one, the state reformatory, to a group of "concerned lifers," men incarcerated without the possibility of parole. In teaching this workshop, I had to be "admitted" to the facility, giving over my belt, credit cards, and identification, taking off my shoes and having them x-rayed while submitting to the possibility of a strip search, proceeding through countless check points and locked doors, skirting the visitors' room filled with sad-eyed women whose toddlers played happily at their feet, proceeding into and across the prison yard while *hundreds* possibly as many as a thousand inmates looked on from behind a three-story chain link fence, some of the prisoners—all felons—standing on the shoulders of others, two to three bodies high, fingers gripping the cage wire, before finally arriving in the Plexiglas-walled classroom where I conducted the workshop without (I did not know this at the time) the presence of a guard. Because of this, one of the most sobering events of my recent life, and the fact that more and more prisons are slated for construction with an eye toward privatization—the Wyoming State Penitentiary in Rawlins had once been privatized—I paid particular attention to any reminiscence authored by or about someone incarcerated, especially in an institution where inmates were required to toil for even the most primitive necessities of life, and took particular note of any relationship he/she might have mentioned concerning a teacher.

All of this is to say, that, given this personal baggage, and given that the above-mentioned events and the above-mentioned abstractions and the above-mentioned young teacher's baby all had at least one common denominator, they were seldom, if ever, directly mentioned in personal reminiscences, letters, or diaries; it was on this premise that the preceding series of linked poems and dramatic monologues found its theme and its title: *We Never Speak of It*.

—Jana Harris
Sultan, Washington
October 2002

MAP/PHOTOGRAPHS

Historical Map of the Western United States Showing Travels and Expeditions of Jim Baker: Scout, Trapper, Indian Fighter, and Famous Guide, 1838–1898, copyright Dr. N. Mumey, Denver, 1931   xi

Outdoor school room, Idaho State Historical Society, #73–215.1   15

Woman in a butcher shop, Idaho State Historical Society, #63–131.5   19

Mother and daughter; Frank Matsura, Washington State University Libraries   23

Young woman driving a four-horse team, American Heritage Center, University of Wyoming   28

Two boys, Frank Matsura, Washington State University Libraries   31

Boy and girl with baby bear, Frank Matsura, Washington State University Libraries   32

Ewe and lamb, American Heritage Center, University of Wyoming   34

Souvenir: Greetings and Best Wishes from Your Teacher, Wyoming State Archives, Department of State Parks and Cultural Resources   37

Little girl holding piglet, titled "Evangeline and Pig." Photo by A.L. Campbell, Oregon Historical Society, #OrHi 74396   39

Roundup crew, Idaho State Historical Society, #79–2.112   46

Visiting the mine, Idaho State Historical Society, #76–207.1   49

Baby's bath, Idaho State Historical Society, #78–160.6   53

Teacher and class, Wyoming State Archives, Department of Parks and Cultural Resources   58

Willow pole cabin, Idaho State Historical Society, #83–94.10   65

Two girls riding donkeys, Wyoming State Archives, State Parks and Cultural Resources   68

Threshing crew's camp wagon, Idaho State Historical Society, #74–56.19   71

Sheep sheering, J. E. Stimson, American Heritage Center, University of Wyoming   75

Rock shelter, American Heritage Center, University of Wyoming   77

Sheep raid, American Heritage Center, University of Wyoming   81

The Zephyr Cabin, Idaho State Historical Society, #73–59.3   83

Bullwhackress, American Heritage Center, University of Wyoming   89

Boy baking bread, Idaho State Historical Society, #77–137.1   93

Girl and her toys, Idaho State Historical Society, #77–81.16   98

Dead baby in coffin, Oregon Historical Society, CN #022064   101

Girls making pioneer snow woman, American Heritage Center, University of Wyoming   110